CW00501218

Learn Fit, Curv _

How to get perfect fit for your curves, even if you know nothing about dressing for your current shape or size

Copyright © 2018 – Rosa Crumpton. All rights are reserved. No part of this guide may be reproduced or transmitted in any form without the written permission of the author, except for the inclusion of brief quotations in a review.

Disclaimer

This guide has been written to provide information to help you create a dream wardrobe. Every effort has been made to make this guide as complete and accurate as possible. However, there may be mistakes in typography or content. Also, this guide contains information on fitting clothing only up to the publishing date. Therefore, this guide should only be used as a guide – not as the ultimate source of fitting clothing.

The purpose of this guide is to educate. The author and publisher do not guarantee that the information contained in this guide is fully complete and shall not be responsible for any errors or omissions. The author and publisher shall have neither liability nor responsibility to any person or entity with respect to any loss or damage caused or alleged to be caused directly or indirectly by this guide.

Material Connection Disclosure

You should assume that the author and publisher have an affiliate relationship and/or another material connection to the providers of goods and services mentioned in this guide and may be compensated when you purchase from a provider. You should always perform due diligence before buying goods or services from anyone via the Internet or offline.

Credits

Many of the images are courtesy of Canva for Work, and most diagrams put together by the author in Canva

Lady Illustration, cover, © Can Stock Photo / V_Gri

Tank top illustration, pg 46, Design Contest

Body Shapes illustration, pg 35, © Can Stock Photo / estherqueen999

Lady illustrations, pg 22, Creative Market / Glanz

Long sleeved top illustration, pg 41, Design Contest

Polo illustration, pg 46, Design Contest

Pants and skirt illustrations, pg 47, Designers Nexus

Message from the Author

Hi, I'm Rosa Crumpton. I love to help women look and feel their very best. I believe that **Style and Grace** is not a Size.

In my 17 years as a member of Zeta Phi Beta Sorority, Inc., I've made more than my share of wardrobe malfunctions, fashion don'ts and wardrobe failures! It's all been a learning experience.

Over the years, I've dedicated time, money and energy into attending New York Fashion Academy, reading as many personal style books, blogs, and resources as possible and spending time helping others.

Have you been going from place to place, door to door, one Google search result after the other, yearning for the solution to your curvy wardrobe challenges?

You have finally been granted your wish—this is the place where all your curvy wardrobe dreams come true.

I am your Curvy Coach and I help smart, busy ladies just like you create the wardrobe of their dreams with **style and grace**.

Let's get started,

Rosa Crumpton
Founder, Soror Style

Contents

Introduction

Hello, I'm Rosa Crumpton, founder of Soror Style, where I help curvy Sorority women look and feel their best. Don't worry if you aren't in a sorority, these tips will help you look and feel your best. I created Soror Style because I want to combine my loves: my Sorority, my knowledge, and experience of the fashion and sewing industry.

I want you to know that it doesn't matter how big or small you are, or if you want to lose weight or not. Wherever you're at right now, this system is going to help you get perfect fitting clothing.

This training is made up of 3 sections. First, we will start with a bit of background from the fashion industry. You'll learn some terminology, some insider tips about the fashion and design process. Learn how clothing goes from an idea to a finished garment that you buy at the store.

In the second section, you will learn the foundations of clothing fit. You'll learn how to get accurate measurements (even by yourself), your body type and figuring out your personal fit challenges. This will give you a really good idea of what's going to work for you and what's not when you go shopping for clothes, saving you lots of time and headache!

The third section is the meat and potatoes of what you'll learn, but please don't skip the other steps. You need a strong foundation to make this system work for you. I'll show you my step by step system for evaluating clothing fit, including online!

So, without further delay, let's get to finding your perfect fit! If you purchased the companion workbook, pull that out too. There will be prompts throughout this book to complete your tasks.

* Complete Pre-assessment in workbook
on page 4 *

SECTION 1

The Challenge Of Great Fit

You may have wondered why it's so darn hard to get clothes that fit your body. This is what I call the challenge of a great fit. So it's not really a conspiracy but clothing is quite literally not made for you.

Originally, clothing was all custom. It was made by either yourself or, if you had the money, someone gifted in clothing making. The beautiful thing about custom clothing is that it is made just for you! Your body, your shape, and your measurements.

After World War II, there were many advances in technology. This made it easier to mass produce items. For clothing, that meant there were now machines that could make tons of clothing in less time than a seamstress could pick out a pattern. This change caused a ripple effect.

One big change was that the cost of clothing went way down. Once clothing began to be mass produced, closets began filling. Since clothing was no longer being made in a one to one model, manufacturers had to design for their ideal body shape and size. Each company began to make their own standards for sizes. In other words, there are no standards when it comes to sizes between companies.

Also, keep in mind that our beautiful bodies are three dimensional, while measurements are not. Two women can have 48" busts and one lady might have a wide back and smaller bust, while the other has a tiny back in comparison and large breasts. A designer may have a set of measurements that seem to fit you perfectly, but that doesn't mean that your body shape and distribution actually fit into their standards. Now let's talk about the actual process of creating clothing.

Fashion Design Process

Having a bird's eye view of the fashion design process will help you get a better clothing fit faster. A designer starts with some inspiration. It could be a color, a season, or even a particular time period. The designer then takes those ideas and continues to brainstorm or start to sketch. Soon, they start to nail down their collection. Once they come up with the clothing that is going to be part of this collection, the designer starts to create technical drawings. Technical drawings are like blueprints for the patternmakers.

Pattern making is a different skill set than fashion design. The pattern maker actually has to translate the designer's ideas into paper pieces that will fit a 3-D body. That's quite a task! Pattern making is part science and part art.

Once the initial draft of the pattern pieces are made, they are used to cut fabric out and create a mockup. This mockup is called a toile or a muslin in designer terms.

Next in the design process is trying on the mockup on a real person. This is a crucial step because just because fabrics can be sewn up in a certain way, it doesn't mean that it will look the way the designer intended on a person. Designers use special people called fit models.

Remember a little while back when I told you clothing manufacturers design for their ideal body size and shape? The fit model tends to be the designer's muse and what the designer sees as their ideal. A fit model is not the same as a runway model. Fit models are usually propriety for that company.

* Complete Fit Model Search in workbook on page 9 *

Back to the design process, the designer checks to see if the design actually translated from the sketch correctly into the fabric.

There may be a few rounds of doing mockups and tweaks before the design is finalized. Once the designer signs off that the garment is finalized, it will go into production.

The next part of the production is grading sizes. Either the original pattern maker or someone else will start to grade from the original size to bigger and smaller ones. So, if the company has a size range 0 through 3x, then they are going to start producing all of those particular sizes.

Pattern grading is another skill. While there are computer programs for patternmaking and grading, nothing beats a skilled person. While a computer program will add or subtract a certain amount from each size, a pattern grader knows that there are certain areas that need more or less change than the standard.

An important step in pattern grading is again making mockups to test out your grading on different sizes. Many companies choose to save money and skip this step, and this can result in clothing that doesn't fit as it should, especially the larger or smaller you get from the original fit model size.

In closing, I just want to remind you that it's not a conspiracy that clothing doesn't fit you. It's just not made for you. But, I don't want you to lose hope. I'm going to give you all the tools, tips and tricks that I possibly can so that you can get a great fit.

Foundations

Let's talk about foundational pieces. Before the term shapewear was popular, there was "foundations." When you're building a house, you need a strong foundation or base before you put the house on top of it. When you build a successful outfit, you need a strong foundation of undergarments.

These undergarments are important because not only do they support your body, they also support the garment structure. They also improve the wear and longevity of the garment. Picture a corset under a strapless gown. The corset keeps the bust lifted as well as giving the gown something to "grip."

Undergarments like slips can help prevent underwear show through, minimize static and it can also increase the longevity of a garment. If you wear a camisole under a blazer, you're going to save money on dry cleaning because you will be able to extend the number of wearings. Your clothing will last longer!

There is a myriad of undergarments. It's easy to get overwhelmed. I'll show you the basics so you can get started.

Spanx™ is probably the most well-known brand of shapewear. They have a full collection of shapewear with levels of control from very lightweight to super heavy duty. Since Spanx™

has so many options, it's a great place to start. Keep in mind there are lots of options if this brand doesn't fit you right.

Types of Shapewear

Let's explore a few types of basic shapewear.

Bra

Bras are probably the most common type of shapewear. A well-fitting bra supports the bust, and depending on the style, they may also shape other areas like the back. A proper fitting bra can visualize shave off several pounds from your silhouette.

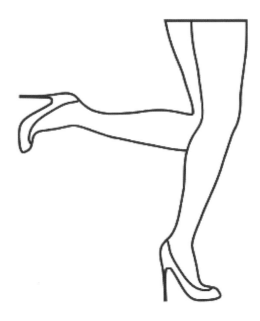

Control top pantyhose or tights

These smooth the entire area, from the waist to toes. Of course, you can also get a legging that's footless. These are available in an almost endless variation of control from very lightweight to super firming. Some styles have control just in the top of the pantyhose and others throughout the entire shapewear.

Camisole/tank

A camisole or tank style shapewear helps smooth everything from the shoulder, through the tummy, to the hip. I find that the ones I like best are the ones that have very low front so that you could wear your best fitting bra with it.

Briefs

Brief shapewear looks like granny panties but these help smooth all the way from their top waistband to your butt and upper thighs.

In the same family, there are shaping shorts. The main difference between briefs and shorts is that shorts have longer legs. They shape and firm all the way from the top waistband through the hips and thighs. These are perfect if you like to wear dresses and skirts and don't have a "thigh gap." This can really help prevent chafing.

Body Shapers/Power slips

Full body shapers or power slips shape and
control several areas at once. They typically shape
from the top of the shoulder all the way down to
the bottom hemline.

Corset/bustier

A corset or bustier is a more specialized type of shapewear. It may also be called a strapless bra. These garments support the bust without straps. They also smooth the area from the bust to the end of the shapewear. These are most commonly needed for strapless types of formal wear. Wedding dresses often require this type of shapewear to support the gown, even if they are not strapless.

* Complete Shapewear Audit, page 10 *

Bra Sizing

The undergarment that is absolutely vital to most curvy women is a properly fitting bra. Even if you are not well endowed in the bust department, a correct fitting bra will make your clothing look better.

Bras sizing is made up of just two measurements. The first is the band measurement taken right underneath your breasts and then the full bust measurement around the largest part of your bust.

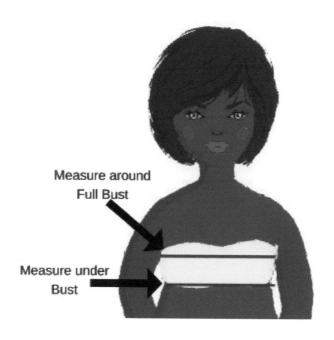

Measure around Full Bust

Measure under Bust

From those two measurements, you get can calculate your cup size, which is just a simple subtraction of your band from your full bust. Whatever the size difference is determines your cup size.

Difference	Cup size
1"	A
2"	B
3"	C
4"	D
5"	DD/E
6"	DDD/F
7"	G
8"	H
9"	I

You would think that since bra sizing only takes two measurements, bras fitting should be easy. I'm sure you're well aware it's not! Some statistics show that over 80% of women are currently wearing the wrong size bra.

There are many reasons why but let me cover a few here. Measurements are, of course, 2D and breasts are 3D. Different manufacturers have different size standards. Just like you learned about in the fashion industry, bra manufacturers use their own fit models and sizes. Then there's the challenge that different fabrics, elastics and trims offer different levels of support. If you've ever lost or gained weight, you know that your bust size can completely change!

Even minimal changes of 5-10 pounds can drastically change the size and shape of your breasts. Many women have never been properly fitted for a bra. And even if we have, we tend to be creatures of habit and just stick with the same size forever!

*Complete Bra Sizing Guide in workbook on page 14 *

Bra Fitting

Once you have the correct size, you can move into bra fitting. The right bra should never be constrictive or dig into your skin. You should be able to move freely without feeling like you can't breathe. It shouldn't leave marks on your body that doesn't go away in a minute or less. A correct fitting bra should not be uncomfortable. Now, keep in mind that if you're not used to wearing the right size, it can take a little while to get used to your new bra.

A well-fitting bra should have cups that fit smoothly over your breasts. There should not be any puckering or gaping. There shouldn't be breast overflow either. All your breast tissues should fit into the cup. It should fit snugly but not too tight. The bra should not be noticeable from the outside of your garment, always think smoothness.

When you find your correct bra, it should fit on the medium hook when new. The reason this is: as you wear the bra, it's going to loosen up over time. Unfortunately, that's just the nature of those elastic fibers that are in the bras. The elastics loosen up with heat and normal wear and tear. Bras do wear out and need to be replaced.

I recommend a professional bra fitting once a year. More often if you have a change in your weight of 5 or more pounds. You may need a fitting if you start taking a medication that changes your hormones, get pregnant or other life events.

The most accurate way to get fitted is to have a professional do it. You can get a professional bra fitting at a large department store or a specialty lingerie store. If you can't do that, try to get somebody else to take your measurements. Last resort is measuring yourself. Now there are ways you can measure yourself, but keep in mind that it is not going to be the most accurate.

If you just absolutely hate bras and know you're never going to wear one, keep reading. There are some other ways that you can get a smooth look. You want to add a layer under your clothing. Items like slips, camisoles, and undershirts can create a much smoother look.

If you hate underwires, give non-underwire bras a try. There are a lot of new styles without underwires that still give nice shaping that will still give you a nice smooth line. Some other options are teddies and non-shapewear bodysuits that will help your clothing lay better. Look for really lovely fabrics—soft, anti-static, and non-cling ones. This will allow your garment to flow on top of it really nicely.

Shapewear guidelines

A general rule of thumb is to use a least restrictive shapewear to get your desired results. Personally, I'm not a big fan of head to toe shapewear for everyday wear. Now, if you like to wear that level of support, more power to you! However, I think as you learn to get perfectly fitting clothing, you may realize you don't need that extra shapewear. I want you to be comfortable so you can handle your daily business!

One thing to keep in mind is the more formal the event, the more supportive your shapewear should be. So, for a red-carpet event, you will likely want more supportive shapewear than say going to a Greek picnic.

Please, please, please, wear your current size in shapewear! I don't want you to be miserable during your whole outing. So, if your shapewear hasn't been worn in a good long time, do yourself a favor and try it on before your event.

SECTION 2

Basics of Fit

At the very core, a good fit is something that makes you look and feel good. It's like the story of Goldilocks and the three bears; it's not too big or too small, it's just right. There shouldn't be any gaping or fabric strain. You shouldn't see any body parts peeking out where they shouldn't!

For a curvy woman, the best fitting clothing just skims over her curves. The clothing doesn't emphasize the wrong curves. To get the best fit, it is likely that you will need to get some tailoring to your clothing. Like with all things in life, there can be too much of a good thing.

Overfitting a garment can happen, when a garment is taken in too much. If it restricts your freedom of movement, then you have overfitted your clothing. This may cause other problems, like wrinkles and fabric strain. Strain on the fabric is not good and it wears out your clothing faster. An important thing to consider when evaluating a garment's fit is the ease the garment was designed to have.

Wearing ease is a term that you may not be familiar with unless you sew. It is the amount of extra fabric width that the designer adds to a garment. The designer determines for a particular style how much extra fabric to add, both for freedom of movement and for the design aesthetic.

Different types of clothing will have different amount of wearing ease built into them. Imagine a thick winter coat. A coat will have extra fabric built into it because it's meant to go over whatever other layers you might be wearing.

Ease in a pair of dress pants is going to be much less since they are not going to be going over extra layers. Where the coat may have 4-5" of ease, the dress pants may only have 1-2", depending on the material and style.

Your personal comfort level and style may call for a little less or a little more ease than what the designer created. There needs to be a kind of balance between the designers intended design and your own comfort level.

Key Areas of Fit

Some key areas of fit to consider is anywhere you have curves. The challenge with fitting clothes for curvy women is that there are just more curves that need to be addressed.

Curvy ladies have bust curves, waist curves (that you may or may not go in), hip curves, thigh curves and others! These can be challenging areas to fit. The type of clothing you are looking to fit will also determine what the key areas are.

For a pair or skinny jeans, the key areas are the thigh and calf measurements, especially if you tend to be on the large or small size in those areas.

No matter your size or shape, we all have our own specific fitting challenges. For example, I'm very busty and also have heavy upper arms. So one of my key areas of fit is the bust and upper arm. For any top I choose, I carefully check the fit throughout the bust and upper arms

Now I want you to think about what your personal fit challenges are. Where are the areas that you have a hard time getting a comfortable fit?

If you're not really sure, go ahead and try on some of your clothes that you never wear. Chances are they probably have some type of fitting challenge. If that doesn't work, you can go window shopping and try on clothing. Take notes on what isn't working.

* Complete Key Areas of Fit in workbook, page 22 *

Measurements

One of the most important steps in getting a perfect fit is accurate, current measurements. Getting these measurements will help you purchase the correct sizes, especially if you purchase clothing online or work with a sewing professional. You will also need the measurement.

It is possible to take your own measurements; however, you will get the most accurate numbers by having someone else measure you. If you don't have a measuring partner, you can find special measuring devices online to help you. Search for "myotape" or "self-measuring tape."

A myotape is a little gadget and you can get it on Amazon or other online stores. It has a little tongue and groove section gear that will snap in and you can take measurements yourself. This tool is good for width measurements but not so great for lengths. To get lengths by yourself, it is usually easiest to measure the lengths of clothing that fits you well.

If someone else is around to take your measurements, you can use a standard sewing measuring tape. It's important to use a sewing one and not some other type. The standard size is a 60 inch. If your largest measurement is around 60" or bigger, get a 96" or 120" measuring tape.

The most common measurements are bust, waist

and hip. You will need these 3 basic measurements to use most body shape calculators. There are many other body measurements you can take. A lot depends on what your key areas of fit are, as well as what type of clothing you usually wear.

General Measurement Tips

It is important to keep your measuring tape nice and even all the way around. For most measurements, you will want to measure around the fullest part of the body. Make sure the tape isn't super tight, and you should be able to fit one finger in between the tape and your body. For these measurements, feel free to round to the closest ½" unless you need these measurements for sewing (then nearest ¼").

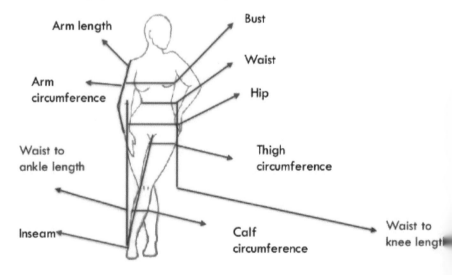

Bust measurement is taken around the fullest part of the bust. Keep measuring tape even and parallel to the floor.

Waist measurement is taken around the smallest part of your middle. Bend to the side if you have trouble finding your waist.

Hip measurement is taken around the fullest part of your butt/hips. Keep the measuring tape even and parallel to the floor.

Arm length is measured from the top of your shoulder to your p bone while arm is softly bent.

Arm circumference is measured around the fullest/fleshiest part of your upper arm.

Inseam is measured from crotch to ankle bone on the   inside   of   your   leg.

Thigh circumference is measured around the thickest part of the upper leg.

Calf circumference is measured around the largest part of the lower leg.

Waist to knee is the length from waist to kneecap, down the side of your body.

Waist to ankle is the length from waist to ankle bone, down the side of your body.

* Complete Personalized Fit Worksheet in workbook, page 23 *

Body Shape

Once you have your measurements taken, it's time to figure out your beautiful shape. Even if you already know your shape, or think you have no shape at all, I challenge you to use your current measurements and see what you get.

There are many schools of thoughts of body shapes. You will find many different names, some after fruits and others after famous people, for example. The number of body shapes also differs depending on who you ask. The most common range seems to be about 4-8 main types.

There are a number of body shape calculators available online. Many of them are free. I have a free calculator available on my website at http://bit.ly/2wAWcvz. Choose your unit of measurement (inches or centimeters) and enter your measurements. In a few seconds, you will be given your result.

Once you have your result, jot that down in your notes. The calculator will also give you suggestions on what clothing will look best for your body shape. You can do some further research and see what type of clothing will flatter your shape best. Be sure to take notes on the information you find.

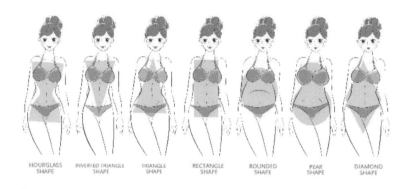

HOURGLASS SHAPE   INVERTED TRIANGLE SHAPE   TRIANGLE SHAPE   RECTANGLE SHAPE   ROUNDED SHAPE   PEAR SHAPE   DIAMOND SHAPE

SECTION 3

Introduction to Evaluating Fit

There's going to be quite a bit of material in this section. First, I'll give you some general tips on evaluating your fit. Then we'll get into my actual process, which I call Fearless Fit Framework (FFF). The FFF is a process I've developed from learning to sew for curvy bodies. This Framework is made up of two main parts. The first Framework covers tops, jackets, and dresses. These types of garments have similar style lines and are very similar in how to evaluate it for fit. The second Framework is how to evaluate pants and skirts.

The best way to evaluate clothing is, of course, in person. I mean actually putting the clothing on, not just holding it up to yourself. No cheating, please! Later, I will give you my tips on evaluating fit for online purchases.

General Tips

It's almost always better to buy something too big than too small. So, if you are in between sizes, your best bet is to go with the larger one. Please don't buy a 5XL if you really wear an XL! When clothing gets way too large compared to you, it will not resize well. Details like pockets and seams will have the wrong proportions. Now don't worry about the size that is printed on the tag, no one will see this, and if it bothers you too much, just cut it out!

The reason to stay close to your true size is it is more accurate. It will also save you on alteration costs if you choose to take it to a sewing professional. A little bit of extra material is easier to take in than to try to create some out of thin air!

Just like pattern making is an art, so too is alterations. Very gifted sewing professionals can create magic and resize just about anything. Just keep in mind that magic costs money. The longer and more complicated an alterations job is, the more expensive it will be.

You always want to use a full-length mirror. Even better is a three-way mirror because you'll be able to see all your angles. If you have an honest friend available, that can be very helpful.

Fearless Fit Framework works in a systematic method. First, you take in the clothing as a whole. Then you start from the top and work your way down in an orderly manner. At first, this may seem overwhelming, but I promise it won't take long to get the hang of it.

You're always going to want to line up your seams, depending on what you're evaluating. The type of garments will determine which seams you need to line up. Generally, these are your shoulder and side seams in the first group, and your side seams in the second group of clothing.

Next, you want to do some light movement. Now, it's great when things fit when you're standing still, but the most important thing in clothing is the fit while you're moving around and living your life.

Then take a few moments to ask yourself some general questions. Does this feel nice overall? Do I even like it? Is it too loose or tight anywhere? Are you seeing any wrinkles or stress points? Is there enough width and length for comfort and movement? Pay special attention to your personal key areas of fit you already identified. You have a busy life and you need to make sure that this outfit is going to be able to handle whatever you need to do before you buy it.

Evaluate Fit in Person

Fearless Fit Framework breaks up garments into two main categories. First, there are tops, jackets, and dresses, and then the second category is pants and skirts. The reason FFF does this is that tops, jackets, and dresses all have similar key areas of fit. Similarly, pants and skirts can be evaluated in much the same way.

FFF allows you to be systematic when you approach evaluating your outfits. You will learn to start from the top and work your way down. You will learn to check all your views front, side, and back. During your evaluation, you will not only make sure that your clothing looks nice from all angles but also that it works for your lifestyle. Learning to evaluate clothing is as much about how things look as it is about the fabrics and that the cut of the garment works for your lifestyle.

Tops/Jackets/Dresses

Let's learn about checking the fit of your tops, jackets, and dresses. The key areas of fit that are similar in these three types of garments are the sleeve, bust, waist, hip, and total length of the garment. Also, you also want to double check those areas that you identified as your personal key areas of fit.

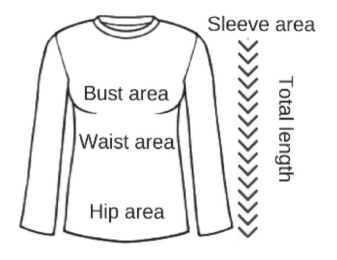

General Guidelines

- Train your eye to figure out where your smallest and largest areas are:
  - The general rule for sleeve length is to have it end at a narrow part
- Long sleeves should always end between your wrist and thumb joint If you're busty, short sleeves should not end at the fullest part of your bust
  - If you're smaller chested, sleeves ending at your full best can help enhance and balance your figure
- The general rule for hemlines are to end at the most flattering area for your body type

The first thing you always want to do is line up your seams. I want you to make sure that the seam lines are lined up anatomically with you to start. The shoulder seam should bisect or cut in half your shoulder. You will want to line that up to where the middle of your shoulder would be. Next, the side seam needs to cut you right in half lengthwise.

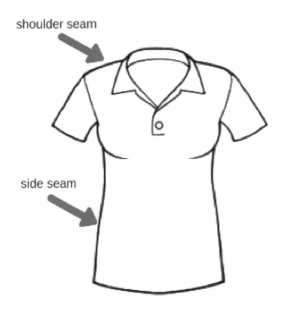

shoulder seam

side seam

Then do some light movements (like stretches) and do a recheck to see if the seams have moved. Ideally, they should relax right back to about where they started. If they don't., this may be a warning sign that alterations will be needed. It could also have to do with the fabric or how the fabric was cut and sewn. File this information in the back of your mind for the time being.

Let's begin at the top. Remember to check all views (front, side, back) when evaluating. First, check the neckline, make sure that it's smooth, that there's no gaping or stretching. This is especially important with a more fitted garment like a jacket or a button up shirt. If your top is sleeveless like this top, you want to make sure that everything is smooth around the armhole. Make sure there is no stretching here. You want to make sure that there is no big space in this area for someone to look down and see your bra.

Now, for garments that have a shoulder, like a t-shirt or jacket, you want to make sure that the sleeve is fitting really nicely into the actual sleeve opening. There should be a nice smooth curve in the top of the sleeve (sleeve cap). There shouldn't be a lot of wrinkling here. Especially in a more tailored garment, like a jacket, the shoulder line shouldn't be sunken in. Most likely, there is a little shoulder pad in there to keep a nice line.

Next, check that you have freedom of movement. Go ahead and do some quick arm exercises by crossing your arms in front of your body and over your head. Make sure you don't see any stress points here when you do this. Next, you want to check your sleeve length. You want to really make sure that it's the right length for you. Take a look at the general guidelines above. If it's too long, you can always get that taken in. Now, if the sleeves are too short, there is not going to be enough fabric. If this is the case, there's not a whole lot you can do. There is a big chance you won't find that matching fabric, but even if you did, you would see a joint of the two pieces of fabric.

Moving on down to your bust area. Take a close look across the fullest part of your bust. Check your front, back, and sides and make sure everything is smooth. This area should cover your curves nicely. If you see a lot of stretching or strain in this area, that means that there's not enough fabric for your bust.

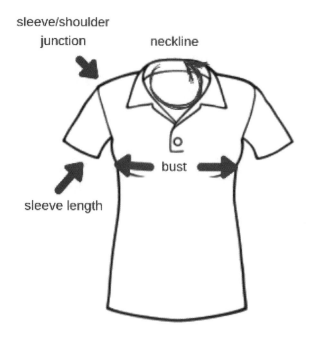

sleeve/shoulder junction   neckline

bust

sleeve length

Then, moving down to the waist area. Make sure it's smooth, that there's not too much fabric (wrinkles). Also, check that it's not stretching out.

Moving down to your hip area, check the same things. Make sure the hip area is smooth and without wrinkles. There should not be a lot of strain or gaping. This is especially true in a button up type of garment. Your garment should be smooth from the top to the bottom.

Whew, we're finally at the bottom your garment. Now it's time to check the length/hemline. It is a good idea to check (especially dresses) with your shoes on. This helps you to ensure the garment is the correct length for when you actually wear it.

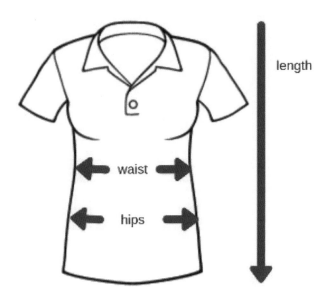

Pants/Skirts

Part two is using FFF to evaluate your pants and skirts. The key areas of fit for pants is the waist, crotch area, hips, back/front view, and of course, the total length. Always double check your personal key areas of fit.

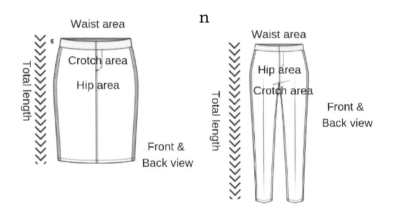

General Guidelines

- The general rule for skirt hemlines are to end at the narrowest part of your leg
- A good rule of thumb for knee length skirts is to end where your calf starts to curve in
- The general rule for pants is to hem so that the front of the shoe is covered and the back is slightly longer but not dragging on the ground
- Cropped pants should end at the narrowest part of the leg

For pants, you will need to line up your seams a little bit different than for tops. Instead of your shoulder seams, you will start with your waist band. Then line up your side seams (inner and outer) if available. Make sure both your outer side seam and your inner side seams lie flat. Depending on the style of the bottom, there may or may not be all of these seams.

Again, do some light movements (like bends or squats) and do a recheck to see if the seams have moved. They should relax right back to about where they started.

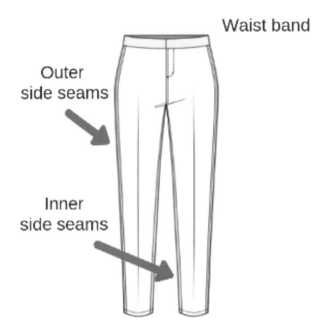

Waist band

Outer
side seams

Inner
side seams

Starting at the top or waistband, we want to make sure that it is straight and even across your waist. Remember to check both the front and back.

Make sure that the waist is smooth without straining, wrinkles, or excess fabric.

Next, evaluate the crotch area (front and back rise); this is more important in pants than in skirts. Check that the crotch length in the front and back is correct. Since your waistband is in the correct position, make sure that there is no fabric strain or extra fabric in this area. If the crotch rise is too short, you will feel the pants pulling up in that area uncomfortably. If the rise is too long, you will see extra fabric bunching up. Keep in mind that it is possible for one rise to be too short and the other to be too long. That's why it's important to do a 360 view of all your angles.

For pants and skirts, the back fit is just as important as the front. Often times when curvy women have the biggest fit issues are in pants, especially in the back. Another thing to keep in mind is the fabric your pants or skirt is made of, especially fitted styles. Some fabrics are really bad about getting stretched out and not snapping back to shape. Within a few hours of wearing them, you will start to see bagginess that you didn't when you originally tried them on. Unfortunately, there is not much to be done about poor fabric except to keep it in mind before you purchase.

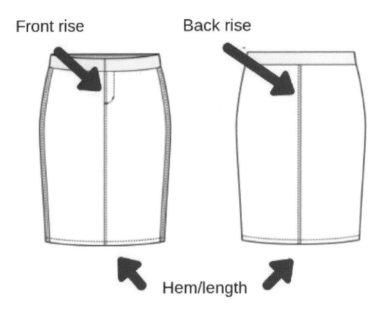

Front   Back

Front rise   Back rise

Hem/length

Lastly, it's time to check the length. Hemlines for pants and skirts are really important. Just like with dresses, please try on with the shoes that you will be wearing. If you don't know the exact shoes, that's ok, just pick your usual height for that type of pants or skirt. If you typically wear flats with pants, then try them on with a pair to get the correct hemline. This is especially true if you choose to take these in to get hemmed by a sewing professional.

So, that is the Fearless Fit Framework system step by step. I know it's a lot of information to learn and it's ok if you feel a little overwhelmed. Just keep at it and the more you practice, the easier and faster this process will be.

Now it's time for you to apply what you just learned. First, I want you to pick your best fitting top and go through the framework, making notes about what you love about it. Second, evaluate your worst fitting top and make notes about what is not working. Next, evaluate your best fitting pants or skirt, again making notes on what's working and what's not working. Lastly, evaluate your worst fitting pants or skirts, noting what is not working.

Now you're armed with vital information moving forward. You will save so much time shopping now that you've worked out your fit!

* Complete Perfect Fit Checklist in workbook
page 35 *

Evaluate Clothing Fit Online

If you're anything like me, you are buying more and more clothing online. I'm going to teach you how to evaluate your online clothing purchases so that you won't be disappointed with them.

Online purchases are always going to be a kind of a guesstimate. But I aim to give you some tips to help you shop online with more confidence. It's really important to rely on the product description and measurements. Now, the quality of this can vary vastly from seller to seller.

You will need to read the clothing description carefully and tease out any clues that are related to fit. This will give you an idea of the ease and what to possibly expect. Make sure that you read each size guide for every piece of clothing. Many times, sizes differ even if it's labeled the same size by the same company. Just make it a practice to pull up the size chart before hitting buy. If you have any questions, reach out to the seller for further guidance.

Pay attention to the measurements, especially if you're ordering from a different country. Double check whether they are using inches or centimeter. You can use an online converter if needed.

Many times, sellers will lay out a garment and measure it flat. This should be clearly communicated. Keep in mind that this is just half of the total width. It's common to see flat measurements on Etsy, eBay, vintage clothing listings, and sometimes manufacturers that customize items like t-shirts. It's easier for sellers to take a flat measurement rather than trying to put on a person or dress for him and figure out what the actual circumferences are. If you see a number that's like 20 inches for the bust of adult clothing, it's a flat measurement or a typo. If it's not clear in the listing, be sure to ask!

Look for keywords in the description that describe the silhouette of the garment. Also, pay close attention to the seams, using the FFF process to look at how the clothing is fitting the model.

Keep your measurements in mind when you are looking to make an online order. You will need to order the size based on your largest measurement. This is the safest bet, although if the fabric is stretched, you may have a little more wiggle room.

Now, do a little online window shopping to test your newly learned skills.

Conclusion

Congratulations! You've made it through the entire Fabulous Fit Framework and it's time to celebrate! You've worked hard to learn how to evaluate your curvy fit. You are on the way to reaping the benefits of finding a perfect fit! Now you have the skills to critically assess your clothing.

These skills will save you heartache from clothing mishaps that aren't wearable. Now that you know what works for you and what doesn't, you can take the next steps of getting your clothing tailored. A sewing professional can help you get a perfect fit.

Ready to learn more?

The Fearless Fit Framework course teaches you how to get a perfect clothing fit for your curves through a series of 4 modules. You'll have instant access to short, to-the-point videos, combined with downloadable guides that will reinforce what you've already learned. Plus, the 4th module will teach you about fabrics and alterations. You will learn how to work with a sewing professional to nail your curvy fit. More information at:

https://www.sororstyle.com/fff-sales-page

Printed in Great Britain
by Amazon

41927300R00030